the english pudding

the english pudding

jane pettigrew

introduction

In households around Britain, as the first course of the family meal is devoured someone at some point will inevitably utter aloud what everyone else is secretly wondering – 'What's for pud?'. Will it be treacle tart with lashings of thick cream? Or apple crumble with ladlefuls of custard? Or steamed chocolate sponge with gooey chocolate sauce? And soon, a most tantalizing clattering in the kitchen tells the eager group gathered around the dining table that something wonderful, scrumptious and heavenly is about to appear.

And the pudding that then takes pride of place on the table is oh, so much more than just the sweet course that ends the meal. It is comfort and home and family and indulgence and contentment and, for each person sharing it, a little slice of a dream come true.

a happy medley of all good things

This wonderful array of antique tableware (right and above) dates from the 18th and 19th centuries and includes Victorian jelly moulds and a copy of a Georgian glass with a barley-sugar-twist stem.

In the 13th century, a poding was a kind of sausage made by filling a skin of animal innards with a mixture of cereals and spiced meat. By the next century, a more refined concoction contained suet, cream, breadcrumbs and spices as well as meat, and was variously spelt poodyng, podding, puddingh or pooddynge.

The Elizabethans replaced the skin pouch with a pudding cloth and cooked a rounder, more solid mass the size of a canon ball, still made of sweet and savoury ingredients. To make 'a light pudding' in the mid 16th century, cooks were instructed to 'take crumes of bread, yolks of egges and cowes milke, with saffron, seeth them together a lytle, as if to make a puddinge'. And 17th-century cookery books told readers that 'it is usual to mix a pudding with flour, eggs, milke, raisins and sometimes both spice and suet, the fat or marrow of meat and several other things … our English pudding is a happy medley of all the good things in the grocer's shop.' In his *Dictionary*, written in 1755, Dr Johnson defined a pudding as 'a kind of food very variously compounded but generally made of meal, milk and eggs'.

In the 18th and 19th centuries, the meat content of the sweeter recipes gradually disappeared; but puddings were still boiled in the same pot as the meat and the vegetables and, although sometimes served at the end of the meal, also acted as fillers during the savoury course to reduce the family's hunger for expensive meat. And in the late 19th century, pudding became what it is today – 'any sweet food served as a dessert', a sweet, luscious, sticky, moreish, satisfying, perfect end to the meal.

sweetmeats and marchpanes

When medieval ladies and gentlemen assembled at long baronial tables for a feast, spread before them was an array of savoury and sweet foods. Among the roasted game birds, the boar's head and spit-roasted 'stekys of venson or bef' were egg custards, junkets, cheesecakes, jellies, apple fritters sprinkled with sugar, and poached fruits in syrup. Flavourings for such sweetmeats included exotic cinnamon, ginger, nutmeg, saffron, cloves and cardamom, discovered through trade with southern Europe.

Each extravagant course of a grand three-course feast comprised some twenty or so platters, and when those had been devoured the servants brought out a 'sotelte' (a subtlety) – an elaborate sculpture representing a naval battle, hunting scene or religious tableau. The structure was often made entirely of sugar, almond paste and jelly, finished in delicate gilding to impress host and guests.

Diners in the 15th century ended their repast by sipping sweet wines and nibbling wafers, nuts, fruits and other sweetmeats. The Elizabethans took great pleasure in cultivating an impressive variety of fruits – quinces, melons, pears, peaches, apricots, cherries, plums, damsons, mulberries and medlars – but preferred not to eat them raw. So pies were baked containing stewed fruit, known as 'tartstuff', flavoured with red wine, spices, sugar and honey. Elizabeth I was presented each New Year by her Master of Pastry with 'a great pye of quinces oringed'. And if Elizabethan revellers were still hungry after such robust dishes, the 'banquet' served as the final course offered candied fruits, biscuits, marmalade and marchpane, which today we know as marzipan.

A selection of boxed Georgian silver 'berry' spoons (right) and an ornate Victorian wire egg basket (below).

the pudding cloth and the englishman's pudding

Kitchen equipment and a Christmas plate dating from the second half of the 19th century. An interest in cookery and the renewed celebration of Christmas were both features of the Victorian era.

The 17th century saw an important leap forward in pudding history with the introduction of the 'pudding cloth' or 'clout', which enveloped the ingredients and held them captive while they boiled away in the family cauldron. To make life easier for the cook, various combinations of suet, breadcrumbs, flour, sugar, milk, eggs, marrow, spices and dried fruits were first worked together in a wooden bowl. The cloth was then laid over the top of the bowl and the entire thing inverted to tip the pudding into its cheesecloth wrap. With the neck of the bag tightly secured with a sturdy piece of string, the firm ball of pudding was lowered into the steaming pot where meat, dumplings and vegetables were already bubbling.

Food writer Sir Kenelm Digby explained in 1670 exactly how to execute this cunning but effective new method of pudding preparation: '... Then put a linen cloth or Handkerchief over the mouth of the dish and reverse the mouth downwards, so that you may tie the Napkin close with two knots; by the corners cross or with a strong thred, upon the bottom of the dish then turned upwards all which is, that the matter may not get out, and yet the boiling water get through the linen upon it on one side enough to bake the Pudding sufficiently. The faster it boils, the better it will be. The dish will turn and rowl up and down in the water, as it gallopeth in boiling. An hours boiling is sufficient.'

This proved such an easy, cheap and efficient way to feed hungry households that the cloth quickly became as essential an item of kitchen equipment as the gridiron and the toasting fork.

a matter of course

In the days of Cromwell and under the Stuart kings, dinner continued to mix meat and fish dishes with custards, almond puddings and fruit pies. In 1662, as a second course to his wedding anniversary dinner, Samuel Pepys enjoyed a 'tanzy' (a sort of egg custard flavoured with the herb of that name), two ox tongues and some cheese. He may of course have then gone on to nibble candied fruit and sugared almonds, for the

Georgian elegance (far right) – a shaped glass bowl, perfect for trifles, and a crisp white linen napkin. The hexagonal pewter plate (right) is from the late 1700s, and the decorative spoon is Victorian.

showpieces of pretty sweetmeats created in Elizabethan times were popular well into the 17th century as the final course to a grand gathering. When he was entertaining the Duke of Beaufort in 1684, Sir Richard Middleton paid out almost £10 for a selection of fruit pastes, candied orange peel, iced cakes, biscuits, almonds, sugar, apples and candied sea holly!

By the end of the 17th century, the sweet dishes that tempted guests hinted at modern favourites and included trifles, cheesecakes, rice puddings and 'white-pots', an early version of bread-and-butter pudding. At this point, Monsieur Misson de Valbourg, French traveller and social commentator, recognized how much the English enjoyed the sweeter parts of their dinner and declared 'Blessed be he that invented pudding!'.

just desserts

Pink junket served in early Victorian copies of Georgian custard cups sitting on a drawn-threadwork tablecloth.

Chefs in the 18th century continued to serve up a jumble of savoury and sweet dishes and the pudding had still not earned a separate role on the dinner table. Admittedly, there was now a clearer division between the first two courses and 'dessert', and French traveller and writer Francois de la Rochefoucauld described how the beautiful, crisp, white linen cloth was removed from the table after the first two courses and 'elegant china baskets' and glass dishes of comfits, candied fruits, sweetmeats, syllabubs, jellies, ices and creams were arranged on the gleaming wooden surface.

The new wealth of the Victorian years brought modern kitchen stoves and gadgets, foreign recipes, new imported ingredients and a hearty appetite for copious quantities of extravagant, robustly satisfying food. The salty and the sugary did still overlap and bills of fare for grand suppers served two courses of mainly savoury platters and a third of such odd mixtures as roasted game birds with jellies, blancmanges, gooseberry tarts, fruit tartlets, cheesecakes and charlottes. Family suppers were more straightforward, with just a small first course, a hearty second and then – hurrah – a pudding! Mrs Beeton's family menus suggested fig pudding, rice pudding, cherry tart, rolled jam pudding and all the puds we still love. So there it was at last – a luscious, scrumptious, heavenly and delicious, proper pudding.

Why does the pudding hold such a special place for us? Perhaps Monsieur Misson summed it up when he said, 'It is a manna that hits the palates of all sorts of people; a manna better than that of the wilderness, because the people are never weary of it.'

school puds

During the hardships and shortages of the post-war 1940s and 50s, cheap filling food was our essential diet. Our mums somehow managed to fill us up with wonderful puddings of every possible type, and we are held in a time warp bestowing us with fond memories of jam roly poly, rice pudding and syrup tart. Government guidelines for school lunches advised: 'In a 4-week period (20 dinners) it is possible to serve 4 milk puddings, 8 steamed or baked puddings of the suet or sponge variety, 4 dishes of stewed, fresh, or dried fruit and custard or fruit in a pudding or pie, 4 pastry dishes.'

School stories by all the favourite children's writers of the time had the occasional scene involving pudding. Enid Blyton starts the new term in her book *The Naughtiest Girl in the School* with the girls sitting down together for a dinner of soup, beef, onions and carrots, dumplings and potatoes, followed by rice pudding and golden syrup. And in Richmal Crompton's *Just William* story, *William's Lucky Day*, due to a scare involving an escaped lion, the Outlaws find a roast-chicken dinner laid out ready on the dining-room table of a nearby house and not a soul in sight to eat it. Needless to say, they tuck in pretty fast, wolf the lot, then William says meditatively: 'Wonder what they were goin' to have after this?' The hatch slides up and there waiting is 'a magnificent cream edifice and a little pile of four plates'. Four gasps of ecstasy go up …. Once the entire pudding has disappeared, Henry speaks for them all when he utters blissfully, 'I feel I wouldn't want to eat another thing for hundreds and hundreds of years.'

The ultimate school pudding – plum duff, served on a frilly plate made in 1740. Below, the puddings in their cloths await steaming.

three hours let it boil

Nothing can beat the sheer heaven and the scrumptious satisfaction of indulgent spoonfuls of steamed syrup or chocolate sponge, plum duff or spotted dick, richly coated in custard and deliciously sweet and sticky.

But would we have enjoyed similar confections in the days when meat, vegetables and pudding were all boiled together in one large black cauldron that hung above the open fire? Admittedly, the 'sweet' part of the meal was separated by the pudding cloth that enclosed it, but the flavours must have mingled to give a stew that tasted of pudding and a pudding that tasted of stew!

As the more affluent Victorians acquired stoves to replace the open hearth, the pudding basin in turn replaced the pudding bag and, at last, savoury remained savoury and the 'sweet' was sweet. Puddings steamed away for hours in their own water in their own pots, retaining their character and marking the division between the two separate courses of the main family meal.

'From the simple suet dumpling up to the most complicated Christmas production … variety in the ingredients is held only of secondary consideration with the great body of people, provided that the whole is agreeable and of sufficient abundance.'

Isabella Beeton, *Book of Household Management* (1861)

steamed chocolate sponge

No suet, only a little sugar, but somehow satisfyingly reminiscent of stodgy, traditional puds. With a fudge or chocolate sauce and cream, quite divine!

100g (4oz) plain flour
1¹/₂tsp baking powder
50g (2oz) cocoa powder
a pinch of salt
50g (2oz) butter, softened
50g (2oz) caster sugar
1 egg, beaten
a little milk

Grease a 1 litre (2 pint) pudding basin. Set a large pan of water to boil. Sift together the flour, baking powder, cocoa and salt and rub in the butter with the fingertips. Stir in the sugar and mix to a dropping consistency with the beaten egg and milk. Pour into the prepared basin. Cover the basin with a circle of greaseproof paper bigger than the diameter of the basin and tie with string. Place in a steamer and set over the simmering water or stand the basin in the pan so that the water comes up to 5cm (2in) below the rim of the basin. Steam for 1–2 hours. Remember to top up the water from time to time. To serve, turn the pudding out onto a serving dish and serve with fudge or chocolate sauce and cream.

'Our five heroes were just devouring the last scrummy morsels of the most enormous stew with doughboys that Bennett had prepared, when Patterson smacked his lips and said, "Capital nosh, Bennett! What's for pud?"'

Jane Pettigrew, *Tuck in Chaps* (1987)

spotted dick

Whereas Spotted Dick is a roll of wickedly stodgy suet dough rolled around a layer of dried fruits, Spotted Dog is made by working the dried fruits into the dough before it is rolled up. In his 1849 *The Modern Housewife*, French chef Alexis Soyer included a recipe called Plum Bolster or Spotted Dick.

350g (12oz) plain flour, sifted
2tsp baking powder
175g (6oz) shredded suet
a pinch of salt
175g (6oz) caster sugar
a little cold water
175g (6oz) mixed raisins, currants
* and sultanas*

Mix together the flour, baking powder, suet, salt and sugar and add enough cold water to bind to a soft but firm dough. On a floured board, roll out to a rectangle approximately 6mm (½in) thick and scatter over the mixture of dried fruits. Dampen the edges with a little cold water and, with the narrow side towards you, roll up. Seal the edges. Wrap in a well-floured pudding cloth and tie the ends. Put into fast boiling water to cook for 2–2½ hours. Remember to top up the water from time to time. Lift out of the water, untie the cloth and turn onto a large, warmed, oval platter. Serve with plenty of custard.

'I never saw anyone enjoy a pudding so much and he laughed
as if his enjoyment of it lasted still.'

Charles Dickens, *David Copperfield*

hot from the oven

As the oven door is opened and a gentle whoosh of hot air carries the first hints of the bubbling golden treat inside, tilt back your head very slightly, close your eyes and breathe in slowly, savouring each moment of promised pudding perfection.

The warm comforting smells of apple pies and rhubarb crumbles are an everyday treat in many a family kitchen. But such pleasures are relatively recent in British culinary history for, although the wealthy have had access to ovens for centuries, our poorer ancestors had to rely completely on toasting forks, cauldrons, spits and griddles. As more and more people could afford a range or stove in the 19th century, baked puddings were adapted from earlier boiled and steamed varieties and were probably rather heavy and indigestible. But chefs and cooks experimented with new cooking methods so that lighter and more appetizing creations were delivered to the table of Victorian families who tucked into fruit tarts, charlottes, batters, dumplings, turnovers and custards. The 20th century added betties and crumbles to the growing choice of cheap, easy puddings that filled us up and sent us from the dining table with sticky mouths, a smile on our faces and a warm, tummy-rubbing sense of satisfaction.

'When baked puddings are sufficiently solid, turn them out of the dish they were baked in, bottom uppermost, and strew over them fine sifted sugar.'

Isabella Beeton, *Book of Household Management* (1861)

eve's pudding

Here is a modern version – unrhymed, unlike the old Sussex recipe below – of this lovely, soft, fruity, lemony, apple sponge pudding.

450g (1lb) apples, peeled, cored
   and roughly chopped
75g (3oz) Demerara sugar
100g (4oz) butter, softened
100g (4oz) caster sugar
2 eggs
100g (4oz) self-raising flour
grated rind of 1 lemon
2tsp freshly squeezed lemon juice
caster sugar for dredging

Preheat the oven to 180°C/350°F/gas mark 4. Put the chopped apples and brown sugar into a pan. Bring to the boil and simmer gently until just beginning to soften. Turn into a pie dish or casserole. In a separate bowl, beat together the butter and caster sugar until light and fluffy. Add the eggs and beat again. Add the flour, lemon rind and lemon juice and beat to a dropping consistency. Spoon the mixture onto the apples and level with a spatula. Bake for 40–45 minutes until golden and firm. Sprinkle the top with caster sugar and serve with custard or cream.

'Then take of the fruit that by Eve was once chosen,
Well par'd and well chopped, at least half a dozen.
Six ounces of bread, let your maid eat the crust.
The crumb must be grated as small as the dust.'

Old Sussex recipe, 1818

jam roly-poly

School dinners in the 20th century left much to be desired, but some of the puddings were yummy. Jam Roly-Poly, known by some with a schoolboy sense of humour as 'sore arm' or 'shirt sleeve pudding', was one of the favourites.

225g (8oz) self-raising flour
a pinch of salt
100g (4oz) shredded suet
90–120ml (6–8tbsp) cold water
4 heaped tbsp jam (raspberry,
  strawberry, black cherry etc)
a little milk
1 egg, beaten
caster sugar for dredging

Preheat the oven to 200°C/400°F/gas mark 6. Grease a baking tray. Sift together the flour and salt. Add the suet and enough cold water to bind and mix to a soft but not sticky dough. Roll out on a floured work surface to a rectangle approximately 20 x 30cm (8 x 12in). Warm the jam in a small saucepan and brush over the rectangle of dough, leaving a 1cm (½in) border all the way round. Brush the border with milk. With the short side towards you, roll up the rectangle of dough and seal the edges carefully. Place the roll on the greased baking tray with the seam underneath. Brush all over with beaten egg and sprinkle with caster sugar. Bake for 40–45 minutes until golden. Serve piping hot with plenty of custard.

apple charlotte

In 1861, Mrs Beeton included in her *Book of Household Management* an 'Easy Method of Making a Charlotte-aux-pommes' and a recipe for 'a very simple apple charlotte'. The first was a sponge-cake case filled with more sponge cake, apple marmalade, sweet wine, whipped cream and apples. The simpler version was a pie-dishful of layers of bread and butter, sliced apples and sugar. All varieties were probably named after Queen Charlotte, wife of George III.

900g (2lb) apples, peeled, cored and sliced
100g (4oz) Demerara sugar
grated rind and juice of 1 lemon
1tsp cinnamon
100g (4oz) butter
8 slices of white bread cut from a large loaf, crusts removed
Demerara sugar for dredging

Preheat the oven to 200°C/400°F/gas mark 6. Use a little of the butter to grease a 1 litre (2 pint) pie dish. Place the apples, sugar, lemon rind and juice, cinnamon and 50g (2oz) of the butter into a pan over a low heat and simmer gently until the apples are soft and the mixture has turned to a purée. Spread the slices of bread with the remaining butter and then cut each slice into 3 fingers. Use some of the bread fingers to cover the bottom of the pie dish and spoon the apple mixture over the top. Cover with the remaining bread fingers and sprinkle the top with the sugar. Bake for 45 minutes–1 hour until crispy and golden on top. Serve hot with custard.

sticky toffee pudding

This Cumbrian original has become a firm favourite all over Britain. It's one of those quintessentially British, marvellously sticky, lip-smacking, insurpassably luscious, comfort puddings.

for the pudding
200g (7oz) dates, pitted
*   and chopped*
1tsp bicarbonate of soda
200ml (8fl oz) boiling water
75g (3oz) butter, softened
150g (5oz) soft brown sugar
2 eggs
175g (6oz) self-raising flour, sifted

for the sauce
100g (4oz) soft brown sugar
200ml (8fl oz) double cream
$1/_2$ tsp vanilla extract
2tbsp butter

Preheat the oven to 180°C/350°F/gas mark 4 and grease a 24 x 10cm (9.5 x 4in) loaf tin. Combine the dates and bicarbonate of soda in a bowl and pour on the boiling water. Leave to stand for 10 minutes. Cream together the butter and soft brown sugar until smooth and light. Beat in the eggs one at a time and then fold in the flour. Add the date liquid and the dates and mix until smooth. Pour the batter into the prepared tin and bake for 45 minutes. Allow to stand for 10 minutes before serving. Combine the ingredients for the sauce in a pan and bring to the boil, stirring. Simmer for 2 minutes. Cut the pudding into slabs, pour over a generous quantity of the sauce and serve with cream or ice cream.

'Sticky toffee pudding ... every bit as gooey as its name suggests.'

The Flag in the Wind

raspberry pudding

As supper was being prepared, the children would be sent down the garden to the raspberry canes to gather a generous bowlful for pudding. The slightly tart freshness of the raspberries melts into the light-as-air sweetness of the sponge topping. No wonder everyone loves this mixture. Sheer summer heaven!

450g (1lb) raspberries
2tbsp caster sugar
2 eggs
1tbsp plain flour
1tbsp caster sugar
freshly squeezed juice of 1 lemon
150ml (5fl oz) double cream

Preheat the oven to 180°C/350°F/gas mark 4. Place the raspberries in a glass dish and sprinkle over the 2tbsp of caster sugar. Separate the eggs. Place the yolks in a small bowl and add the flour and 1tbsp of caster sugar. Mix well. Add the lemon juice and cream and mix again. Whisk the egg whites until stiff and fold into the egg yolk mixture. Spread the mixture over the raspberries and bake for 20–25 minutes until golden and firm. Serve warm with lots and lots of cream.

'The proof of the pudding is in the eating
The proof of a woman is in making the pudding
The proof of a man is in being able to appreciate both.'

From an old Sussex recipe book

custards, flawnes and a foole or two

Fools, rather like trifles, have become the names of desserts because they are mere follies or light insubstantial things; Victorian soufflés involved a good deal of whisking by hand 'to a strong froth'; syllabubs descend from Elizabethan party pieces made by taking milk direct from the cow into a jug of ale, wine or cider to make a bubbling, frothy, alcoholic cream; and custards, over the centuries, have varied from solid baked confections set in a pastry case to soft, creamy, pouring sauces flavoured with vanilla, almond or brandy. John Taylor's *Feast* of 1638 instructed: 'To furnish a Feast compleatly, there must be Tarts, Custards, Flawnes, Flap-jackets, and by al meanes a Foole or two.'

The Elizabethans loved a good joke and a favourite at celebration dinners (and very popular at the Lord Mayor's Feast) was 'The Almaine Leap into a Custard'. 'A vast dish, broad and deep, was filled with custard and placed on the table and, while the company was busily employed …, a Zany, or Jester, suddenly entered the room and, springing over the heads of the astounded guests, plunged himself into the quivering custard, to the unspeakable amusement of those who were far enough away from the tumbler not to be bespattered by the active gambol.'

little chocolate puddings

Who can resist a rich chocolate finale to a wonderful meal? These individual fondant ramekins of gooey, melting chocolate combine the satin-smoothness of a chocolate mousse with the light airy texture of a steamed chocolate sponge and are delicious.

200g (7oz) diced butter
200g (7oz) dark chocolate, broken into pieces
2tbsp brandy
100g (4oz) golden caster sugar
4 large eggs, plus 4 large egg yolks
1½ tsp vanilla extract
50g (2oz) plain flour, sifted

Grease 8 x 150ml (5fl oz) ramekins or mini pudding basins. Place the butter, chocolate and brandy in a bowl over a pan of simmering water until melted. Stir until glossy. Place the sugar, eggs, egg yolks and vanilla in a large mixing bowl and whisk until doubled in volume, thick and frothy. Add the melted chocolate mixture by pouring it around the edge of the bowl and then sprinkle the flour over the top. Slowly and carefully fold in with a metal spoon. Divide the mixture between the prepared ramekins. Cover and put in the fridge for at least 2 hours or up to 8 hours. Heat the oven to 200°C/400°F/gas mark 6. Bake the puddings for 12 minutes until risen. Remove from the oven. They will sink slightly. Serve hot.

'All I really need is love, but a little chocolate now and then doesn't hurt!'

Lucy Van Pelt (in 'Peanuts', by Charles M. Schulz)

gooseberry and elderflower fool

The addition of cream and rich custards to stewed fruit creates a velvet smooth pudding out of otherwise plain and perhaps sour ingredients. Gooseberries are almost always too hard and acid to eat uncooked and unsweetened, and Isabella Beeton advised, when making gooseberry fool, to 'put in plenty of sugar, or it will not be eatable'. She recommended the dish for May and June, saying, 'This, although a very old-fashioned and homely dish is, when well made, very delicious, and if properly sweetened, a very suitable preparation for children.'

To create a slightly lighter version of a traditional fool, substitute the cream with crème fraîche or thick Greek yogurt or use a mixture of cream and crème fraîche.

450g (1lb) gooseberries
5tbsp granulated or brown sugar
4tbsp elderflower cordial
5tbsp water
300ml ($^1/_2$ pint) double cream
small curls of lemon zest to
  decorate
a few mint leaves for garnishing

Top and tail the gooseberries and put into a pan with the sugar, elderflower cordial and water. Bring gently to the boil and simmer for about 10 minutes until soft and juicy. Allow to cool. Put the gooseberries through a food processor or mash with a potato masher. Do not sieve. Spoon the pulp into a bowl. Whip the cream until it just begins to form soft peaks and fold into the gooseberry puree. Spoon into one large serving dish or into individual glass dishes. Decorate the top with curls of lemon zest and mint leaves.

vanilla egg custard

A recipe book from the 16th century instructed that 'To make a Custarde, the coffyn must be fyrste hardened in the oven, and then take a quart of creame and five or syxe yolks of egges, and beate them well together, and put them into the creame, and put in sugar and small raysyns and Dates sliced, and out into the coffin butter or els marrowe, but on the fyshe daies put in butter.'

Custard pies are still very popular but so too are custards without the pastry – just soft, vanilla-flavoured moments of joy, melting on the tongue and satisfying our craving for sweet, lazy pleasure.

4 eggs
600ml (1 pint) full-fat milk
350g (10oz) caster sugar
a few drops of good-quality vanilla essence
freshly grated nutmeg for sprinkling

Preheat the oven to 160°C/325°F/gas mark 3. Put the eggs, milk, sugar and vanilla essence into a bowl and place it over a pan of simmering water. Beat until the mixture is hot and then pour into 6 ramekins. Sprinkle the top with a little nutmeg. Stand the ramekins on a baking tray and bake for 40 minutes until set.

'Though we eat little flesh and drink no wine, yet let's be merry, we'll have tea and toast; custards for supper and an endless host of syllabubs and jellies and mince pies, and other such ladylike luxuries.'

Percy Bysshe Shelley (1792–1822)

syllabub

A 1792 recipe from the *London Art of Cookery* gave these instructions for making the perfect syllabub: 'Put into a punch bowl a pint of cider and a bottle of strong beer. Grate in a small nutmeg, and sweeten to your taste. Then milk from the cow as much milk as will make a strong froth. Then let it stand an hour, strew over it a few currants well washed, picked and plumped before the fire, and it will be fit for serving.'

The traditional flavouring for a syllabub is white wine and lemon juice but this version made with Grand Marnier and oranges is light, frothy and slightly intoxicating with a refreshing citrus kick.

2tbsp Grand Marnier
grated zest and juice of 2 medium
*   oranges*
300ml (¹/₂ pint) double cream
2 egg whites
50g (2oz) caster sugar
curls of orange zest to decorate

Mix together the Grand Marnier, orange zest and juice. Whisk the cream until stiff and then gradually whisk in the Grand Marnier mixture. Beat until well incorporated. Whisk the egg whites until stiff and then whisk in the sugar. Fold the egg whites into the cream and blend carefully. Spoon into individual glass dishes and decorate with curls of orange zest.

more than mere trifles

Summertime, and it's too hot for suet puds or piping hot pies! Instead, it's time for jellies moulded Victorian-style into fantastic shapes, for melting meringues with whipped cream and red berries, for trifles and summer puddings, fruit salads and ice creams.

Jellies and fruits have always played a part on the dining table. At medieval banquets, diners were served sweet jellies, custards, tarts and poached fruits. Elizabethan guests retired after dinner to the banqueting house to indulge in preserved fruits, jellies, tarts, fools and sweet wines.

Sir James Caldwell recorded that in October 1772, guests at Castle Ward in County Down were fed a 'second course of nine dishes … The cloth was taken away and then the fruit – a pine apple, not good; a small plate of peaches, grapes, and figs (but a few) and the rest, pears and apples.'

By the mid 19th century, dinner 'à la française' consisted of three courses and dessert, which included such treats as 'Charlotte aux Pommes', 'Gelee aux Fraises', 'Creppes Froides', apricot tart, rice blancmange and 'sweet omelet'.

'Trifles make perfection, but perfection is no trifle.'
Michelangelo (1475–1564)

eton mess

This wonderful summer indulgence originated at Eton College in the 1930s, when bowlfuls of whipped cream, sugar and chopped fruit were served in the school's tuck shop. The meringue chunks are a later addition and the dessert became the special treat enjoyed by boys and parents at the annual 4th of June prize-giving picnic.

for the meringues
3 large egg whites
¹/₂ tsp cream of tartar
150g (5oz) caster sugar

for the 'mess'
450g (1 lb) strawberries
600ml (1 pint) double cream
1 rounded tbsp caster sugar

To make the meringues, lay baking parchment on a baking tray. Preheat the oven to 120°C/250°F/gas mark ½. Whisk the egg whites until frothy and foamy. Add the cream of tartar and beat until the mixture holds soft peaks. Add the sugar a little at a time and continue beating until really stiff. Drop neat spoonfuls onto the baking tray and bake for 1 hour, occasionally turning the tray, until the meringues are ivory-coloured and firm. Switch off the oven and leave the meringues inside to cool. To make the mess, whiz 250g (8oz) of the strawberries in a food processor and sieve to remove the pips. Cut the remaining strawberries into halves (or quarters, if very large). Break the meringues into chunks. Whip the cream until just beginning to thicken, add the sugar and fold in the puréed and chopped strawberries and the meringues to give a marbled effect. Serve in individual dishes.

port wine jelly

Victorian cookery writers recommended port wine jelly as nourishing food for recovering invalids. Made with isinglass to set it and flavoured with a little grated nutmeg, lemon and sugar candy, nursing staff or parents were instructed 'Two wineglassfuls is enough at a time. It is best taken warm. If taken cold, a spoon of course must be used.' Jellies like this are perfect nursery food – they simply dissolve and fill the mouth with a fruity burst of flavour.

2tbsp gelatine or a vegetarian substitute
300ml (1/2 pint) water
thin strips of orange zest
50g (2oz) caster sugar
a pinch of nutmeg
250ml (8fl oz) red port
freshly squeezed juice of 1 orange
grapes and cherries to garnish

In a small bowl or cup, mix the gelatine with a little of the water, stand the bowl or cup in a pan of hot water and allow the gelatine to dissolve. Put the remaining water, the orange zest, caster sugar and nutmeg into a pan and heat gently to dissolve the sugar. Remove the pan from the heat and stir in the port and the orange juice. Strain the mixture through a sieve and pour into individual glass dishes or a jelly mould. Chill in the fridge until set. Decorate with grapes and cherries.

'... *in such cases also jellies of all colours ... in such representation of sundry flowers, herbs, trees, forms of beasts, fish, fowl and fruits ....*'

Description of England 1587, by William Harrison, Essex Rector

summer pudding

The upturned mound of scarlet midsummer fruits marries the favourite shape of a British winter pudding with an explosion of sunshine flavours. In the 1950s and 60s, the pudding was usually turned out into a serving bowl and surrounded by a solid moat of bright yellow custard. Today, juicy wedges are served with generous ladlefuls of lightly whipped cream, pouring cream or a lighter blend of cream with crème fraîche or thick Greek yogurt.

225g (8oz) redcurrants
100g (4oz) blackcurrants
225g (8oz) strawberries
225g (8oz) raspberries
150g (5oz) caster sugar
8 slices fresh white bread, crusts removed

Wash the currants and remove the stalks. Pick over the strawberries and raspberries and remove stalks and any bruised areas. Put all the fruit into a pan with the sugar and simmer gently for 4–5 minutes over a low heat until the sugar has dissolved and the juices start to run from the fruit. Remove the pan from the heat. Keeping back 1–2 slices for the lid, use the bread to line a 1 litre (2 pint) pudding basin, overlapping the slices to make a secure case for the fruit. Pour the fruit and juice into the basin and cover the top with the remaining bread. Place a saucer or small plate over the bread and place a heavy weight on top of that to press the pudding down in the basin. Place in the fridge for at least 6 hours or overnight. To serve, turn the pudding out into a serving dish, cut into wedges and serve with cream.

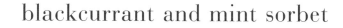
blackcurrant and mint sorbet

From the Turkish word '*sherbert*' (fresh drink) came our name for frozen mixtures of fruit and sugar, and sorbets are said to have become popular long before we learned to make ice cream. Before refrigeration, ice for preserving food and preparing frozen desserts was taken from ponds and rivers in the bitter chill of winter, or delivered by wagon and stored in special brick-lined pits or cellars. The first recorded ice house in England was built at Greenwich in 1619 and the first iced dessert is said to have been eaten at Windsor Castle in 1677. Those early ices were made by burying tin icing pots containing fruit and cream mixtures in pails of broken ice.

150ml (5fl oz) water
6–8 fresh mint leaves
225g (8oz) soft brown sugar
750g (1lb 11oz) blackcurrants
fresh mint leaves to serve

'*At desserts, or at some evening parties, ices are scarcely to be dispensed with.*'

Isabella Beeton, *Book of Household Management* (1861)

Bring the water to the boil, pour over the fresh mint leaves and leave to infuse for 10 minutes. Strain the liquid into a large pan and discard the leaves. Add the sugar to the liquid and heat gently to dissolve the sugar. Add the blackcurrants, bring to the boil and simmer for 5 minutes. Cool and put through a food processor, then sieve to remove the pips and skins. Freeze the mixture in an ice-cream machine. If you don't have an ice-cream machine, freeze the liquid in a tray and when just solidified, mash with a fork and freeze again. When frozen, blend until smooth, cover and refreeze. Serve decorated with fresh mint leaves.

ginger ice cream with a mango coulis

It is said that the Chinese tucked into ice creams and sorbets hundreds of years ago, and certainly Marco Polo experienced the treat while travelling through their land in the 13th century. And Roman Emperor Nero is said to have had snow brought down from the mountains to freeze his festive drinks. A hand-cranked machine for making iced puddings was invented in 1846 in America and commercial production started in 1851.

for the ice cream
200ml (7fl oz) full-fat milk
3 egg yolks
50g (2oz) caster sugar
300ml (¹/₂ pint) double cream
3 egg whites
3 large knobs of crystallized root
  ginger, chopped
1–2tbsp of the syrup from the
  jar of ginger
2tbsp ginger wine

for the mango coulis
2 cans mango pulp or 2–3 large
  mangos, de-stoned and skinned
caster sugar to taste

Bring the milk slowly to the boil in a heavy pan. Beat together the egg yolks and sugar until thick. Pour the hot milk into the egg mixture, stirring continuously. Pour the mixture back into the pan and simmer gently until the custard thickens enough to coat the back of a wooden spoon. Do not allow to boil. Leave the mixture to cool. Whisk the cream until stiff and the egg whites until stiff. Fold the cream, egg whites, chopped ginger, ginger syrup and ginger wine into the custard. Turn the mixture into an ice-cream machine or pour into a freezer-proof container, cover and freeze until firm. When ready to serve, whiz the mango pulp in a blender or food processor and sweeten to taste. Spoon the ice cream into individual glass dishes and trickle the coulis over the top or to the side.

58

the nursery and beyond

It seems that many of our favourite modern puddings evolved from 'pottage' – the staple food of the Romans and Saxons. This mess of cereals, meats, vegetables, dried fruits and spices was obviously so confused by its oddly schizophrenic blend of ingredients that it could not decide which route to follow. So gradually, it split in two and headed off in different directions, turning itself along one road into savoury soups, stews and suet-encrusted meat pies and along the other into sweet milky porridge, boiled suet puddings filled with fruit, blancmanges, mincemeat, plum puddings and cakes.

In medieval Britain, rice and other imported grains were too expensive for the ordinary workers but the wealthy enjoyed almond-flavoured rice pottages on high days and holy days. To make the plain mixtures of milk with rice, sago, tapioca or semolina more enticing, cinnamon or nutmeg were added, butter, eggs and cream gave a thicker, more luxurious consistency, and plumped-up dried fruits lent texture and flavour. In childhood, we dolloped bright red jam into our bland but nourishing milk puddings and called the result 'Accident in the Alps', and our early enjoyment of these creamy and comforting dishes in the nursery lends a note of nostalgic pleasure each time we tuck into them today.

'What is the matter with Mary Jane?
She's perfectly well and she hasn't a pain,
And it's lovely rice pudding for dinner again!
What is the matter with Mary Jane?'

A.A. Milne, *When We Were Very Young* (1924)

crème brulée

This is much much richer and creamier than other custards and has a brittle sugary lid. Before grills and kitchen blow-torches were invented, chefs used a 'salamander' – a sort of pudding branding iron, heated over the fire and placed over the sugary topping to melt and brown it. At Trinity College, Cambridge, this piece of equipment was used to scorch the college crest into the top of the cream, giving the pudding its alternative name of 'Trinity Cream'.

Has anyone ever found the perfect crème brulée or has the search turned into a life quest?

for the brulée
4 egg yolks
1tbsp caster sugar
600ml (1 pint) double cream
a few drops vanilla essence

for the topping
caster sugar

Preheat the oven to 140°C/275°F/gas mark 1. Beat the egg yolks and sugar together. Warm the cream in a heatproof bowl over a pan of simmering water. Pour into the egg mixture and stir well. Place the bowl back over the pan and beat gently until the mixture is thick enough to coat a wooden spoon. Add the vanilla essence, mix well and pour into individual ramekins. Place in a baking pan containing 2.5cm (1in) water. Bake for 30–40 minutes, then remove from the oven and leave to chill overnight. To serve, sprinkle caster sugar 0.5cm (¼in) thick over the custard. Place the ramekins under a very hot grill as close to the heat as possible. The sugar will melt, brown and bubble.

crème caramel

Despite its chic French name, this egg custard is a descendent of
Welsh medieval 'flummery', Chaucerian 'blankemange' and Tudor
'flaune'. Many nations have their own version – in Spain it is 'flan',
in France, 'crème renversée' and in Italy, 'crema caramella'. The
caramelized sauce and silky smooth cream create a flavour that you
want to hold in your mouth for much longer than is possible.

75g (3oz) caster sugar
1tbsp cold water
2 eggs plus 2 egg yolks
2tbsp caster sugar
a few drops vanilla essence
600ml (1 pint) milk

Preheat the oven to 180°C/350°F/gas mark 4. Gently
melt the 75g of caster sugar in a pan until it becomes
liquid and changes colour to a rich dark brown. As it
starts to bubble, add the cold water, mix and pour into
the base of a soufflé dish. Move the dish around to
spread the caramel evenly. Whisk together the eggs,
yolk, sugar and vanilla essence. Bring the milk to just
below boiling point and pour onto the egg mixture.
Pour into the soufflé dish and stand in a roasting tin
with water that comes halfway up the sides of the tin.
Bake in the middle of the oven for 35–40 minutes.
Cool, then turn out onto a serving platter or dish.

baked in a pie

Mrs Isabella Beeton declared firmly in 1861 that 'pastry is one of the most important branches of culinary science. It unceasingly occupies itself with ministering pleasure to the sight as well as the taste …', by which she was referring to the spectacle of all the intricate sculptures and elaborate adornments devised by the Victorians to decorate their pies.

Centuries before, the Elizabethans had also relished a good pie, turning a sweet or savoury item on the menu into a paste-enveloped party piece. Dwarfs or children were hidden inside large pies, flocks of birds were entombed, live frogs were enclosed croaking in a 'coffyn' of pastry that was carved and gilded, painted and embellished with leaves, flowers and heraldic motifs. Then, at a strategic moment in the revelling and feasting, a sharp knife sliced through the outer layer to free the joke inside.

When the Bishop of Glastonbury decided to send King Henry VIII a Christmas gift, he chose his steward, Jack Horner, to deliver a novelty pie containing the title deeds to twelve manorial estates in England. On the way to visit the king, Horner lifted the pastry crust and helped himself to the 'plum' of the properties, the Manor of Mells in Somerset. It is said that his descendants still live in the house today!

'Little Jack Horner sat in the corner
Eating his Christmas pie.
He put in his thumb and pulled out a plum
And said, "What a good boy am I!"'

Traditional nursery rhyme

lemon meringue pie

A good lemon meringue pie should have the crumbly texture of the pastry mingling with the sharp, smooth lemon filling and tantalizing the mouth with the meringue's light, frothy frivolity.

225g (8oz) ready-to-use
shortcrust pastry

for the filling
4tbsp cornflour
300ml (¹/₂ pint) cold water
25g (1oz) butter
grated rind and juice of 2 lemons
2 eggs, separated
175g (6oz) caster sugar

'The fresh rind of the lemon is a gentle tonic and, when dried and grated, is used in flavouring a variety of culinary preparations.'

Isabella Beeton, *Book of Household Management* (1861)

Preheat the oven to 200°C/400°F/gas mark 6. Grease an 18cm (7in) round flan dish. On a floured board, roll the pastry out to a 25cm (10in) circle and line the flan dish. Trim the edges, line the base with greaseproof paper, add a layer of baking beans and bake blind for 15–20 minutes. Remove the beans and paper and bake for a further 5 minutes. Remove from the oven and allow to cool. Reduce the oven temperature to 160°C/325°F/gas mark 3. In a small pan, blend the cornflour with a little of the water. Add the remaining water and mix well. Add the butter and bring to the boil, stirring constantly. Cook for 3 minutes, stirring. Remove from the heat and add the lemon rind and juice, egg yolks and 50g (2oz) of the caster sugar. Pour the mixture into the pastry case. Whisk the egg whites until very stiff. Add 50g (2oz) of the remaining sugar and whisk again. Fold in the remaining sugar. Spread the meringue over the filling and bake for 20–25 minutes until the meringue is set and pale golden. Serve warm or cold.

bakewell tart

This Derbyshire pudding is said to have been invented by accident at the White Horse Inn in Bakewell when the landlady asked a new and somewhat inexperienced kitchen assistant to make a strawberry tart. The poor would-be chef left the sugar and eggs out of the pastry and used them instead to make a topping that she spread over strawberry jam instead of fresh strawberries.

Some recipes top the jam with a custard made with eggs, butter, sugar and ground almonds, while one or two old versions also add cold mashed potato (rather like the mixture that went into old English curd cheesecakes such as Maids of Honour).

225g (8oz) ready-to-use
shortcrust pastry

for the filling
4tbsp good-quality raspberry jam
50g (2oz) butter, softened
50g (2oz) caster sugar
1 egg
a few drops almond essence
40g (1½ oz) ground almonds
15g (½ oz) self-raising flour

Grease and line a shallow 18cm (7in) round sandwich tin. On a floured board, roll out the pastry to a thickness of approximately 6mm (¼ in) and use to line the prepared sandwich tin. Preheat the oven to 190°C/375°F/gas mark 5. Spread the jam over the pastry base. For the topping, beat together the butter and sugar until light and fluffy. Add the egg and beat well. Add the almond essence, ground almonds and flour and mix well. Spoon the mixture over the jam and smooth with a palette knife. Bake for 30 minutes until firm and golden. Serve warm or cold with custard or cream.

cherry pie

For the cockneys of London, a 'Cherry Pie' is rhyming slang for 'a lie'! But for pudding addicts it is a glorious burst of flavours – the sweetness of golden pastry, the almond of cherry kernels and the plump ripeness of rich red cherries.

550g (1lb 2oz) ready-to-use
  puff pastry

for the filling
900g (2 lb) ripe cherries, pitted
275g (10oz) caster sugar
25g (1oz) plain flour
1tsp almond essence
50g (2oz) butter
caster sugar for dredging

Preheat the oven to 200°C/400°F/gas mark 6 and grease a 22.5cm (9in) shallow pie dish or plate. Roll out half the pastry to fit the pie dish or plate. Line the dish and trim the edges. In a bowl, combine the pitted cherries, sugar, plain flour and almond essence and turn into the pastry shell. Dot with butter. Roll out the remaining pastry to a circle big enough to cover the pie, moisten the edges with a little water or milk and lay over the dish. Trim the edges and press the rim firmly down onto the bottom layer of pastry. Make two or three short slits in the centre of the pastry to allow any steam to escape and bake for 40–50 minutes until golden. Sprinkle the top with caster sugar.

'The last cherry soothes the roughness of my palate.'

Robert Browning (1812–1889)

apple pie

During his travels around Scotland in 1773, Samuel Johnson made copious notes as to the food and drink he enjoyed. On a visit to St Andrew's University, he reported: 'The professors who happened to be resident in the vacation made a public dinner, and treated us very kindly and respectfully.' Dinner consisted of 'salmon, mackerel, herrings, ham, chicken, roast beef, apple pie.' Jane Austen wrote that 'Good apple pies are a considerable part of our domestic happiness' and most pudding lovers would probably agree.

750g (1lb 10oz) ready-to-use shortcrust pastry

for the filling
2kg (4lb) slightly tart eating apples, peeled, cored and thickly sliced
3–4tbsp soft brown sugar (or more or less to taste)
1tsp mixed spice or grated nutmeg caster sugar for dredging

Grease a 20cm (8in) pie dish. Preheat the oven to 180°C/350°F/gas mark 4. Divide the pastry into two. On a floured board, roll out one half and use to line the pie dish. Trim the edges with a knife. Arrange the apples over the pastry and sprinkle with the sugar and spice. Roll out the remaining half of the pastry. Moisten the edges with a little water or milk and place the second circle over the top. Press down on the pastry edges, making sure that they are properly sealed, and trim off any excess pastry. Cut two or three short slits in the centre of the pastry to allow any steam to escape and bake for 40–45 minutes until golden. Sprinkle the top with caster sugar.

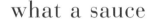

what a sauce

Cream and crème fraîche and ice cream make any pudding special, but sometimes we want a change. Here are some yummy sauces that will add an extra scrumptiousness to dessert.

4 eggs
100g (4oz) caster sugar
600ml (1 pint) milk
a few drops of vanilla essence

real custard For serving hot with crumbles, charlottes, steamed puds, baked puds, pies and tarts.

Beat the eggs with the sugar in a heat-proof bowl and add the milk and vanilla essence. Put the bowl over a pan of simmering water and stir until the custard begins to thicken. Do not allow it to boil, or it will instantly curdle.

175g (6oz) caster sugar
300ml (½ pint) water
50g (2oz) cocoa powder
a pinch of ground cinnamon

pouring chocolate sauce For pouring over steamed chocolate pudding.

Put the sugar and water into a pan and stir over a gentle heat until the sugar has melted. Bring to the boil and simmer for 1–2 minutes. Stir in the cocoa powder and cinnamon and bring back to the boil, stirring all the time so that it doesn't burn. Serve hot or warm.

100ml (4fl oz) double cream
25g (1oz) unsalted butter
500ml (20fl oz) water
25g (1oz) soft brown sugar
juice of ½ lemon

fudge sauce For pouring over ice cream, chocolate pudding or steamed puddings.

Heat the cream, butter, water, sugar and lemon juice in a pan for 3–4 minutes, stirring all the time so that it doesn't burn. Serve hot or warm.

cooked in books

William Shakespeare, so wise about all aspects of the human condition, must have known that the English would develop a passion for sugar, chocolate, pudding and other sweet indulgences. In *A Midsummer Night's Dream* he suggests, 'A surfeit of the sweetest things the deepest loathing to the stomach brings.' But yet, some of his characters obviously enjoy such pleasures. Richard III declares, 'When I was last in Holborn, I saw good strawberries in your garden there. I do beseech you send for some of them.' But in *Troilus and Cressida*, Shakespeare recognized that other pleasures were important and perhaps more enduring: 'But still sweet love is food for fortune's tooth.'

Billy Bunter, created by Frank Richard, always overindulged, and excelled himself in *Bunter Comes for Christmas*. '"Ooooh!" moaned Bunter.

"Wooooh! I say, you fellows – Ooooh! Wooooh! I- I don't feel well, really I don't. Ooooh! Can't you stop cackling. Don't know what you're laughing about. Ooooooh!"' Although Bunter and friends were sympathetic, there was little they could do for a fat owl when 'four helpings of turkey were on bad terms with seven of Christmas pud, and all of them at war with a dozen or more mince pies'.

Charles Dickens' Christmas, as it happens in *A Christmas Carol*, of course includes the essential seasonal end to the festive dinner in the shape of '... the pudding, like a speckled cannon-ball, so hard and firm, blazing in half of half-a-quartern of ignited brandy, and bedight with Christmas holly stuck into the top.'

But it is Oliver Twist who sums it up for all of us pudding lovers: 'Please Sir, I want some more.'

acknowledgements

The publishers wish to thank The Dining Room Shop, 62-64 White Hart Lane, Barnes, London SW13 0PZ for the loan of photographic props for this book, with special thanks to David Hur for allowing the use of some of his personal items.

Quotations are reproduced as follows:

page 18, the quote from *William's Lucky Day* by Richmal Crompton, copyright ©A.P. Watt Ltd on behalf of The Executors of the Estate of Richmal Ashbee, reproduced with permission

page 34, the quote from *The Flag in the Wind,* reproduced with permission of The Scots Independent

page 40, the quote by 'Peanuts' character Lucy Van Pelt, copyright ©United Feature Syndicate, Inc., reproduced with permission

page 60, the quote from 'Rice Pudding' from *When We Were Very Young* by A.A. Milne, copyright ©The Trustees of the Pooh Properties, reproduced with permission of Curtis Brown Group Ltd, London

page 78, the quote from *Bunter Comes For Christmas*, copyright ©Frank Richards, reproduced with permission